# PEARLS
# WISDOM

# PEARLS *of*
# WISDOM

*A Collection of Inspirational Quotes*

**BRITISH MUSLIM HERITAGE CENTRE**

First Edition, 2022

British Library Cataloguing-in-Publication Data
A catalogue-in-Publication record for this book is available from the British Library

ISBN: 978-1-9164041-3-7

Hadiths compiled by: Nasar Mahmood & Shafiq Siddiq

Hadith verification by: Shaikh Anis Gouissem

Design by: Shafiq Siddiq

Published by:
British Muslim Heritage Centre
College Road
Whalley Range
Manchester
M16 8BP

Website: www.bmhc.org.uk • Email: info@bmhc.org.uk

BRITISH MUSLIM HERITAGE CENTRE

# Introduction

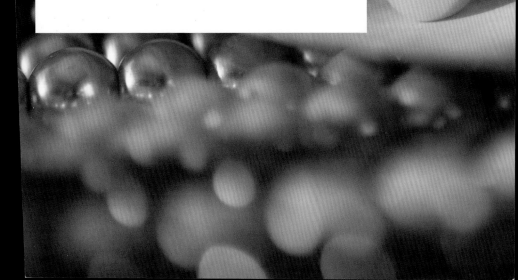

*Words have the power to influence others, whether it's to get something done, to learn or teach, to change the world, or sometimes, just to make us feel better.*

*The pearls of wisdom uttered by the Prophet of Mercy, Muhammad (peace be upon him), are among the timeless, unforgotten words that continue to resonate with us today. They have the ability to move us deep inside and evoke hope, love, justice, compassion, kindness, self-reflection, courage, and also effect social change.*

*We hope some of the timeless quotes we have compiled in this book will continue to inspire a new purpose and outlook in our lives.*

**British Muslim Heritage Centre**

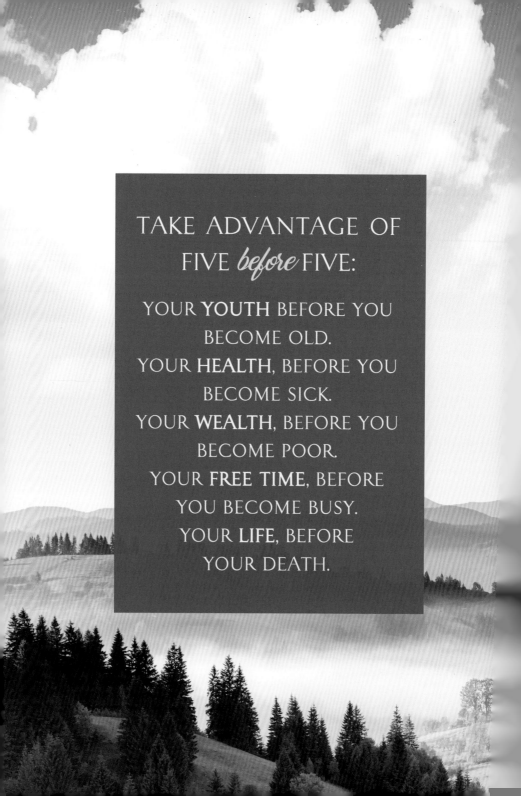

TAKE ADVANTAGE OF
FIVE *before* FIVE:

YOUR **YOUTH** BEFORE YOU
BECOME OLD.
YOUR **HEALTH**, BEFORE YOU
BECOME SICK.
YOUR **WEALTH**, BEFORE YOU
BECOME POOR.
YOUR **FREE TIME**, BEFORE
YOU BECOME BUSY.
YOUR **LIFE**, BEFORE
YOUR DEATH.

THE STRONG PERSON IS NOT SOMEONE WHO HAS A LOT OF PHYSICAL STRENGTH, RATHER THE STRONG PERSON IS SOMEONE WHO CAN CONTROL THEMSELF IN ANGER

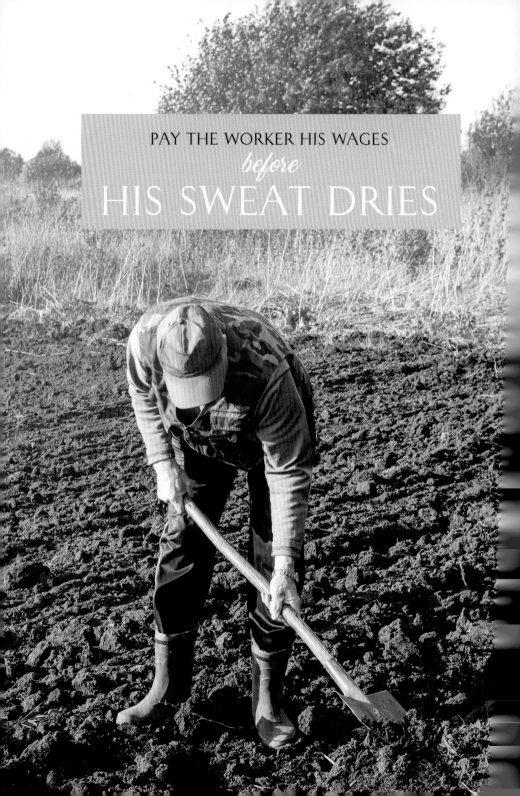

PAY THE WORKER HIS WAGES
*before*
# HIS SWEAT DRIES

*Gentleness*

DOES NOT ENTER
ANYTHING EXCEPT
THAT IT BEAUTIFIES IT,
AND HARSHNESS
DOES NOT ENTER
ANYTHING EXCEPT
THAT IT DISFIGURES IT.

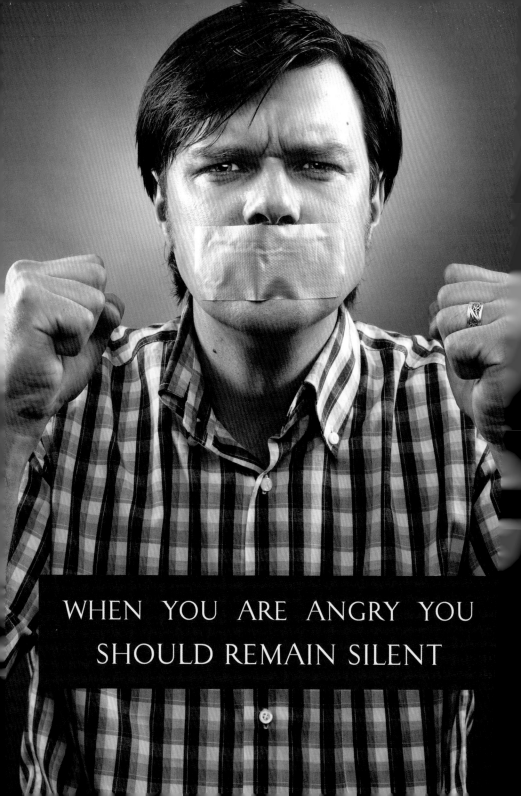

WHEN YOU ARE ANGRY YOU
SHOULD REMAIN SILENT

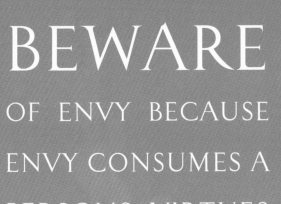

# BEWARE

OF ENVY BECAUSE
ENVY CONSUMES A
PERSONS VIRTUES
JUST AS FIRE
CONSUMES
FIREWOOD.

# THERE IS A REWARD FOR
## *Kindness*
# TOWARDS EVERY
# LIVING THING

# BEWARE

OF SUSPICION,
FOR SUSPICION
IS THE WORST
OF FALSE TALES.

FULFILL THE TRUST TO THE
ONE WHO ENTRUSTED YOU
AND DO NOT CHEAT THE
ONE WHO CHEATED YOU.

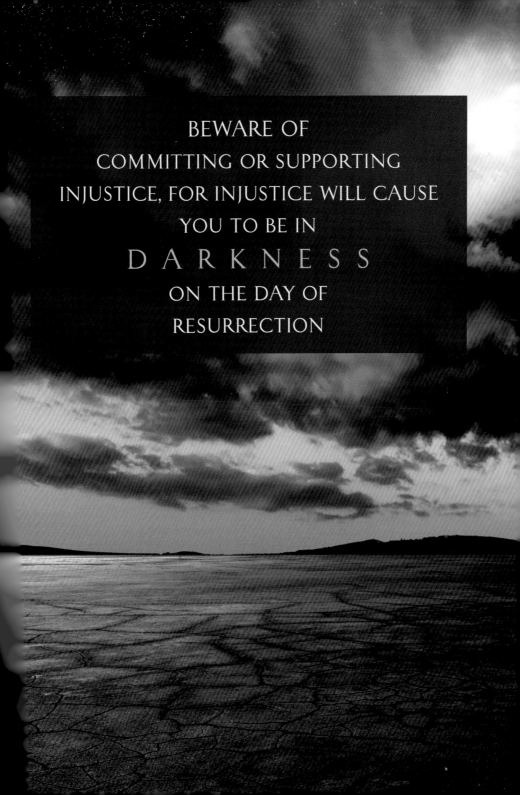

BEWARE OF
COMMITTING OR SUPPORTING
INJUSTICE, FOR INJUSTICE WILL CAUSE
YOU TO BE IN
D A R K N E S S
ON THE DAY OF
RESURRECTION

SPREAD *peace* AND YOU
WILL RECEIVE *peace*

DO NOT WASTE WATER
EVEN IF YOU ARE AT A
RUNNING STREAM

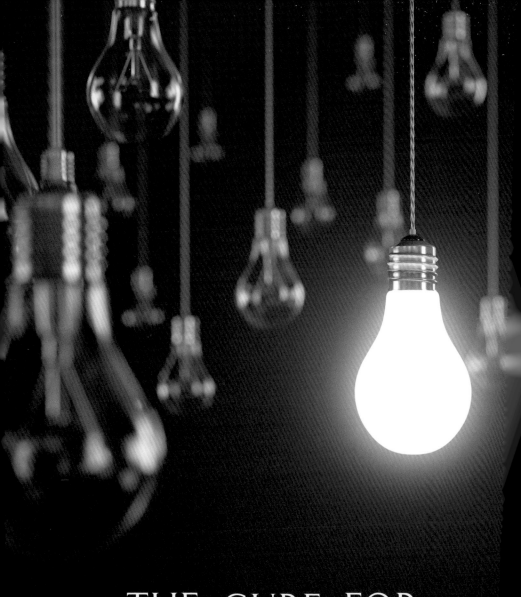

# THE CURE FOR IGNORANCE IS TO QUESTION

WEALTH IS NOT
HAVING MANY
POSESSIONS.
RATHER TRUE
WEALTH IS THE
RICHNESS
OF THE SOUL

THE *best* ARE THOSE WHO *help* OTHERS THE MOST.

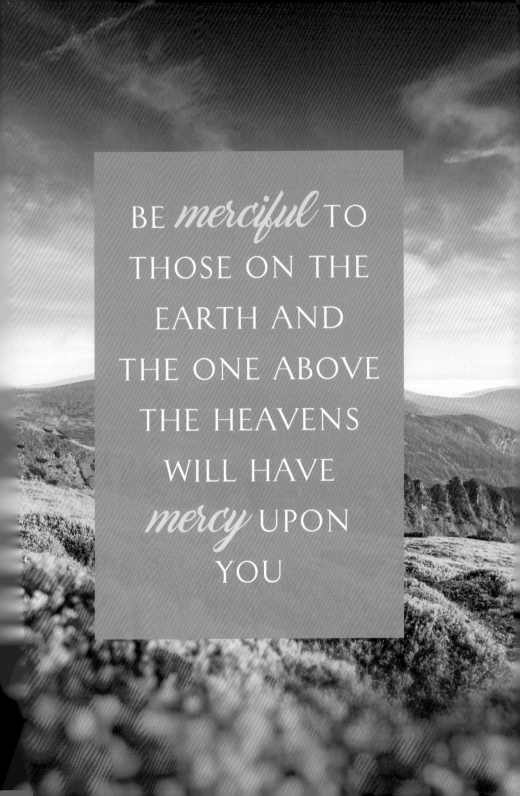

THEY ARE NOT FROM US
WHO DO NOT SHOW
MERCY TO THE YOUNG
OR RESPECT THOSE
WHO ARE OLD.

REMEMBER GOD IN TIMES OF
*ease*
AND GOD WILL REMEMBER YOU IN TIMES OF
DIFFICULTY

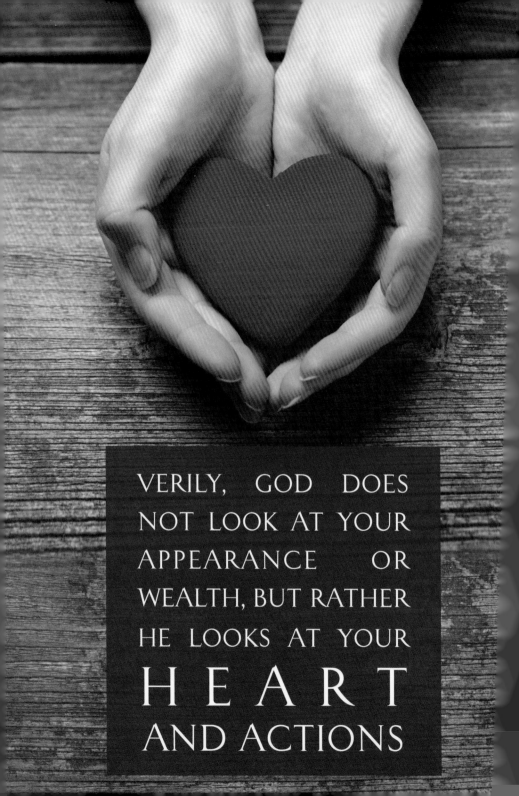

VERILY, GOD DOES NOT LOOK AT YOUR APPEARANCE OR WEALTH, BUT RATHER HE LOOKS AT YOUR **HEART** AND ACTIONS

THE MOST PERFECT IN FAITH
AMONGST THE BELIEVERS IS HE
WHO IS THE BEST IN
MANNERS
AND KINDEST
TO HIS WIFE.

IF YOU HEAR OF AN OUTBREAK OF PLAGUE IN A LAND, DO NOT ENTER IT; BUT IF THE PLAGUE BREAKS OUT IN A PLACE WHILE YOU ARE IN IT, DO NOT LEAVE THAT PLACE.

HE IS NOT A
BELIEVER
WHO FILLS
H I S
STOMACH
WHILE HIS
NEIGHBOR
G O E S
HUNGRY

*Love* FOR OTHERS
WHAT YOU *Love*
FOR YOURSELF

DO YOU KNOW WHAT IS BETTER THAN FASTING, PRAYER AND CHARITY? IT IS KEEPING GOOD RELATIONS BETWEEN PEOPLE, AS QUARRELS AND BAD FEELINGS CAUSE DESTRUCTION.

DO NOT BELITTLE ANY ACT OF KINDNESS, EVEN THAT OF GREETING OTHERS WITH A *smile*

A GOOD DEED DONE TO AN ANIMAL IS AS MERITORIOUS AS A GOOD DEED DONE TO A HUMAN BEING, WHILE AN ACT OF CRUELTY TO AN ANIMAL IS AS BAD AS AN ACT OF CRUELTY TO A HUMAN BEING

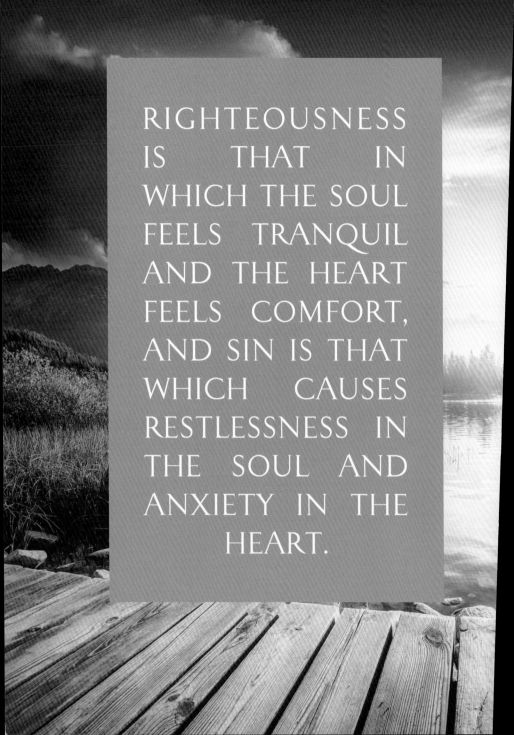

RIGHTEOUSNESS IS THAT IN WHICH THE SOUL FEELS TRANQUIL AND THE HEART FEELS COMFORT, AND SIN IS THAT WHICH CAUSES RESTLESSNESS IN THE SOUL AND ANXIETY IN THE HEART.

WHOEVER IS NOT GRATEFUL FOR THE
SMALL THINGS
WILL NOT BE GRATEFUL FOR THE
LARGE THINGS.
WHOEVER DOES NOT THANK
PEOPLE, HAS NOT THANKED
GOD ALMIGHTY.

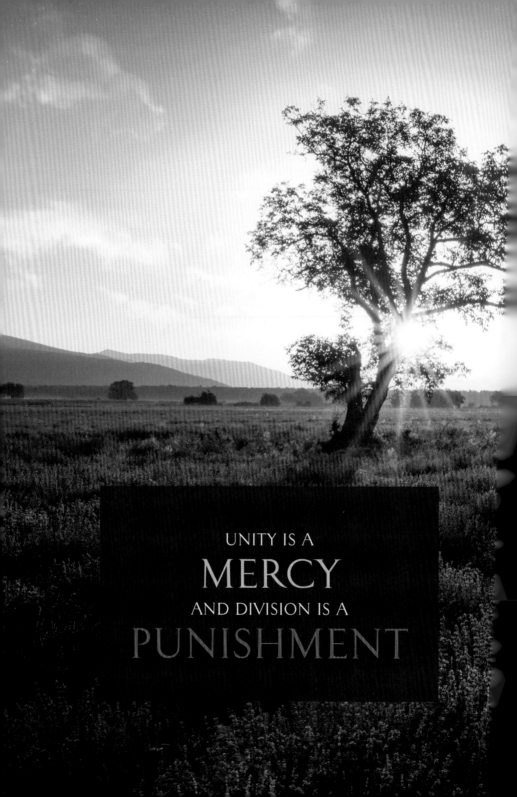

UNITY IS A
MERCY
AND DIVISION IS A
PUNISHMENT

A WHITE PERSON HAS NO SUPERIORITY OVER A BLACK PERSON, NOR DOES A BLACK PERSON HAVE ANY SUPERIORITY OVER A WHITE PERSON. YOUR SUPERIORITY IS ONLY ON THE BASIS OF YOUR PIETY.

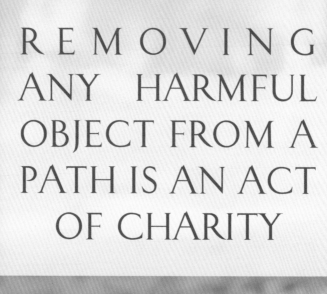

REMOVING ANY HARMFUL OBJECT FROM A PATH IS AN ACT OF CHARITY

ONE ADOPTS THE WAY OF HIS
FRIEND
SO BE CAREFUL IN SELECTING YOUR
FRIENDS

THE COMPANY OF GOOD FRIENDS
IS LIKE WALKING INTO A SHOP OF
PERFUME. WHETHER YOU BUY THE
PERFUME OR NOT, YOU ARE BOUND
TO RECIEVE THE FRAGRANCE.

TWO BLESSINGS THAT MANY OF
THE PEOPLE WASTE ARE

HEALTH
&
FREE TIME

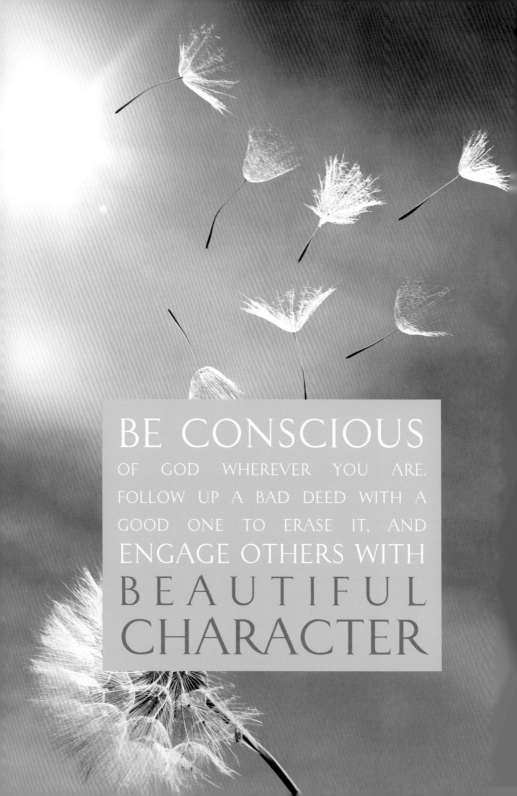

BE CONSCIOUS OF GOD WHEREVER YOU ARE. FOLLOW UP A BAD DEED WITH A GOOD ONE TO ERASE IT, AND ENGAGE OTHERS WITH BEAUTIFUL CHARACTER

# THE RULES OF
# WAR

DO NOT KILL ANY CHILD, WOMAN OR OLD PERSON.

DO NOT KILL MONKS IN MONASTERIES, AND DO NOT
KILL ANYONE IN ANY PLACE OF WORSHIP.

DO NOT DESTROY VILLAGES AND TOWNS, AND DO
NOT SPOIL CULTIVATED FIELDS AND GARDENS.

DO NOT BETRAY TRUSTS OR COMMIT MUTILATION.

DO NOT BURN OR CUT DOWN ANY TREES.

DO NOT DESTROY ANY INHABITED PLACE.

HE WHO TRULY BELIEVES IN GOD
AND THE LAST DAY SHOULD SPEAK

*good*

OR REMAIN

SILENT

# WHAT SOME FAMOUS HISTORICAL FIGURES HAVE SAIDABOUT MUHAMMAD

*"I have studied him – the wonderful man and in my opinion far from being an anti-Christ, he must be called the Saviour of Humanity.*

*I believe that if a man like him were to assume the dictatorship of the modern world he would succeed in solving its problems in a way that would bring it the much needed peace and happiness: I have prophesied about the faith of Muhammad that it would be acceptable to the Europe of tomorrow as it is beginning to be acceptable to the Europe of today."*

## - Sir George Bernard Shaw

*Sir George Bernard Shaw was an Irish playwright, literary critic, polemicist, ? activist and winner of the Nobel Prize Literature in 1925.*

*"I became more than ever convinced that it was not the sword that won a place for Islam in those days in the scheme of life. It was the rigid simplicity, the utter self-effacement of the Prophet. The scrupulous regard for pledges, his intense devotion to his friends and followers, his intrepidity, his fearlessness, his absolute trust in God and in his own mission."*

- **Mahatma Gandhi**

*Mahatma Gandhi was an Indian lawyer, anti-colonial nationalist and political ethicist who employed nonviolent resistance to lead the successful campaign for India's independence.*

"*The founder of twenty terrestrial empires and of one spiritual empire that is Muhammad. In regards to all standards by which human greatness may be measured, we may well ask, is there any man greater than he?*"

- **Alphonse de Lamartine**

*Alphonse de Lamartine was a French poet, and statesman who was instrume the foundation of the French Republic.*

*"My choice of Muhammad to lead the list of the world's most influential persons may surprise some readers and may be questioned by others, but he was the only man in history who was supremely successful on both the secular and religious level."*

- **Michael H Hart**

*Michael Hart is an astrophysicist, author, and professor of astronomy, physics and the history of science.*

"No other religion in history spread so rapidly as Islam. The West has widely believed that this surge of religion was made possible by the sword. But no modern scholar accepts this idea, and the Qur'an is explicit in the support of the freedom of conscience.

Like almost every major prophet before him, Muhammad fought shy of serving as the transmitter of God's word sensing his own inadequacy. But the Angel commanded, "Read". So far as we know, Muhammad was unable to read or write, but he began to dictate those inspired words which would soon revolutionise a large segment of the earth, "There is one God."

- James A. Michener

James A. Michener was an American who wrote more than 40 books, many were bestsellers. He was known for the meticulous research that went into his

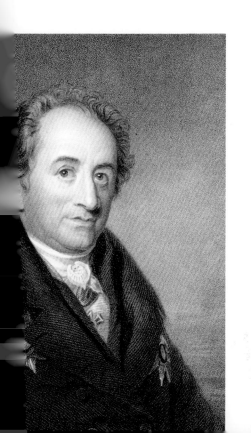

"*We Europeans with all our concepts and ideas have not yet attained that which Muhammad attained, and no one will ever surpass him. I searched in history for the loftiest example for man to follow, and I found it in the Prophet Muhammad. Thus the truth must prevail and become supreme, because Muhammad succeeded in subjugating the whole world by means of the message of Divine Oneness.*"

- **Goethe**

*Goethe was a German poet, playwright, novelist, scientist, statesman and critic. He is considered to be the greatest German literary figure of the modern era.*

"*His readiness to undergo persecutions for his beliefs, the high moral character of the men who believed in him and looked up to him as leader, and the greatness of his ultimate achievement – all argue his fundamental integrity. To suppose Muhammad an impostor raises more problems than it solves. Moreover, none of the great figures of history is so poorly appreciated in the West as Muhammad.*"

- **William Montgomery Watt**

*William Montgomery Watt was a S Orientalist, historian, academic an Anglican priest.*

"... he was Caesar and Pope in one; but he was Pope without the Pope's pretensions, and Caesar without the legions of Caesar. Without a standing army, without a bodyguard, without a palace, without a fixed revenue, if ever any man had the right to say that he ruled by a right Divine, it was Muhammed; for he had all the power without its instruments and without its supports."

- **Reginald Bosworth Smith**

*Reginald Bosworth Smith was a renowned English schoolmaster and author.*

P O E M

# MUHAMMAD
## A MERCY TO MANKIND

A man who taught mercy, kindness and duty;
A man who repelled evil with virtue and beauty.

A man who brought forgiveness and inspired the truth;
A man who dispelled racism and was never aloof.

A man who sought justice and the end of oppression;
A man who was forbearing through trial and repression.

A man who loved orphans and supported the weak;
A man who gave life to the rights that we seek.

A man with compassion and loving grace;
A man who smiled at every face.

A man who affirmed and taught God's Divinity;
A man who inspired hope and endless serenity.

A man who was upright, honest and kind;

He was the Prophet Muhammad, a mercy to mankind.

*"And We have not sent you, [O Muhammad],*
*except as a mercy to the worlds."*

The Qur'an
Chapter 21, Verse 107

# References

1. *Take advantage of five before five. Your youth before you become old. Your health before you become sick. Your wealth before you become poor. Your free time before you become busy. Your life before your death.*
[Al-Hakim, Shu'ab al-Iman, 9767]


2. *The stronger person is not someone who has a lot of physical strength, rather the strong person is someone who can control themselves in anger.*
[Sahih al-Bukhari, 6114 & Sahih Muslim, 2609]


3. *Pay the worker his wages before his sweat dries.*
[Sunan Ibn Majah, 2443]


4. *Gentleness does not enter anything except that it beautifies it, and harshness does not enter anything except that it disfigures it.*
[Sahih Muslim, 2594]


5. *When you are angry you should remain silent.*
[Musnad Ahmad, 2137]


6. *Beware of envy because envy consumes a persons virtues just as fire consumes firewood.*
[Sunan Abu Dawood, 4903]

7.   *There is a reward for kindness towards every living thing.*
[Sahih al-Bukhari, 2466]

8.   *Beware of suspicion, for suspicion is the worse of false tales.*
[Sahih al-Bukhari, 6064]

9.   *Fulfil the trust to the one who entrusted you and do not cheat the one who cheated you.*
[Sunan al-Tirmidhi, 1264]

10.   *Beware of committing or supporting injustice, for injustice will cause you to be in darkness of the Day of Resurrection.*
[Al-Adab Al-Mufrad, 488]

11.   *Spread peace and you will receive peace.*
[Musnad Ahmad, 18059]

12.   *Do not waste water even if you are at a running stream.*
[Sunan Ibn Majah, 425]

13.   *The cure for ignorance is to question.*
[Sunan Abu Dawood, 336]

14. *Wealth is not having a lot of possessions. Rather true wealth is the richness of the soul.*
[Sahih al-Bukhari, 6446 & Sahih Muslim, 1051]

15.   *The best are those who help others the most.*
[al-Mu'jam al-Awsat, 5937]

16.   *Be merciful to those on the earth and the one above the heavens will have mercy upon you.*
[Sunan al-Tirmidhi, 1924]

17. *They are not from us who do not show mercy to the young or respect those who are old.*
[Musnad Ahmad, 7073]

18. *Remember God in times of ease and God will remember you in times of difficulty.*
[Sunan al-Tirmidhi, 3382]

19. *Verily, God does not look at your appearance or wealth, but rather He looks at your heart and actions.*
[Sahih Muslim, 2564]

20. *The most perfect in faith amongst the believers is he who is the best in manners and kindest to his wife.*
[Sunan at-Tirmidhi, 1162]

21. *If you hear of an outbreak of a plague in a land, do not enter it, but if the plague breaks out in a place while you are in it, do not leave that place.*
[Sahih al-Bukhari, 5728]

22. *He is not a believer who fills his stomach while his neighbour goes hungry.*
[al-Sunan al-Kubra, 19049]

23. *Love for others what you love for yourself.*
[Sahih al-Bukhari 13 & Sahih Muslim, 45]

24. *Do you know what is better than fasting, prayer and charity? It is keeping good relations between people, as quarrels and bad feelings cause destruction.*
[Sunan al-Tirmidhi, 2509]